BY HIS LIGHT

I WALKED THROUGH THE DARKNESS

a Memoir

KAREN WELCH ADKINS

CLAY BRIDGES
PRESS

By His Light I Walked through the Darkness
A Memoir

Published by Clay Bridges in Houston, TX
www.ClayBridgesPress.com

ISBN: 978-1-953300-01-0
eISBN: 978-1-953300-03-4

Special Sales: Most Clay Bridges titles are available in special quantity discounts. Custom imprinting or excerpting can also be done to fit special needs. Contact Clay Bridges at Info@ClayBridgesPress.com.

*To my beloved Bill, the man of my dreams.
Thank you for giving me such a beautiful life and
making all my dreams come true. I will always
love you.*

*To my late parents, Otis and Kathryn Welch, who
raised me as a child of God and taught me the
ways of the Lord.*

*To my sweet brothers, Mel and Dean, who beat
me to heaven. Soon we will all be together again.*

*To my brother-in-law, Pastor Randy Brewer, who
always made me laugh. He went to be with the
Lord three months before Bill.*

*To my sons Johnnie, Alan, and Jake, their wives,
and my grandchildren for all their love for me
and patience with me through this life-altering
event.*

Special Thanks

Special thanks to my Lord and Savior Jesus Christ for the things He has done in my life, for giving me the opportunity and ability to minister his word. I love you, Lord, with all my heart, soul, mind, and strength.

Table of Contents

Foreword

There is a hard truth that most people who have lived life know but never want to face.

I have been in public ministry along with running businesses and organizations for close to 40 years. I've been traveling the world, breaking bricks with my head, bending steel in my teeth, and snapping police handcuffs. My life has included building youth ministries, leading the world-famous Power Team, and founding Team Impact with our own TV show, which aired in 260 countries for more than 20 years. I have seen well over a million people stand at our altars to accept

Jesus as their Lord and Savior. And now, I'm pastoring a wonderful multiple-campus church.

In all that I have had to deal with the hard truth that has hit many people's lives many times, the hard truth manifest in many forms and fashions. It is relentless and has no real boundaries that contain it.

The hard truth is this: Life is difficult, and there are not always easy solutions. "How frail is humanity! How short is life, how full of trouble!" (Job 14:1 NLT).

I met Bill Adkins and his wonderful wife, Karen, a couple of decades ago. One glaring truth in my early relationship with them is that they were the center of each other's worlds. Bill would address Karen as Baby Girl, and she always saw him as that tall handsome cool drink of water. Yes, they were in love, and it showed.

They had learned another truth of life, and that was to pull all the beauty, love, memories, laughter, fun, and wonderfulness of family out of life. And that's exactly what they always tried to do. Bill had a singing voice and a love for the Lord that was unequaled or unparalleled unless it was Karen with her love and commitment.

Our relationship intensified when I was leading Team Impact and traveling the world. Their church fell into a calamity and was in need. The local church body had a battle to face, difficult times, and hard choices. Bill had privately spoken to me about what he felt was needed and how these things could be worked through for the strengthening and healing within the body of the local church. So I started commuting from Dallas to Crosby, Texas, about a four-hour drive. I would often get there on Wednesday, speak that night, stay in the back of the church, preach on Sunday, and then head back to Dallas after the morning service. We did that routine for about a year. I use the word *we* because the Adkins family was all in.

Karen and Bill would lead worship, and oh, what worship it was! It was always at a whole new level of connection and exchange.

During this time, two or three times a week, I would ride a Harley (my good friend Prentice Alexander lent it to me) to Bill and Karen's home, and we would sit at their kitchen table and talk, plan, pray, dream, and believe God into the future. These times would end up usually around 2:00 a.m. or 3:00 a.m., and then I would leave. Bill would take an hour or so nap and have to head out to work.

Those will always be treasured moments in my life. I saw such a depth of Karen and Bill's heart and love for the Lord. Before the Lord, the decision was made, and I came to pastor Crosby Church. My wonderful wife, Lorie, and I joined Bill and Karen to serve the Lord in ministry as a team for the next 15 years. What a ride it was through the highs and lows, peaks and valleys. We were a team through and through.

There is such a strength in Karen, her heart and compassion for the things that are right, her loyalties, and her love for her husband and three boys—Johnnie, Alan, and Jake. Wow! These boys were sure a handful. Then the grandbabies came next.

Then the diagnosis—an aggressive brain tumor. Could this be true? What would be next? Well, we all walked through it, and the strength and faith that Karen walked in every day for the next 14 months were evidence that God is able to do exceedingly abundantly more than we could ever think, ask, or imagine.

By His Light I Walked through the Darkness is a powerful story of life lived well. It is an inspiration to us all, regardless of the circumstances. Yes, it is the ability to take this gift of life that God has given us and use every ounce of it to the fullest in family, friends, laughter, relationships, and building memories and a lasting lineage that moves generations to come.

By His Light I Walked through the Darkness will inspire any reader to a full understanding of what God can do regardless of a situation or circumstance. You are not a victim or collateral damage; you are an overcomer, not an undergoer. You will be taken on a whirlwind of the adventures of a lifetime. Karen shares her hurt and pain but also her victories and triumphs. She will take you on a journey that may bring tears but also laughter. So enjoy, press in, and you will be blessed.

To my great friend, Bill, I miss you. Thank you for your love and integrity of life. Looking forward to the time when we worship together again. Love you, my brother.

Keenan Smith
Lead Pastor, Crosby Church
Cofounder, Team Impact Ministries
Businessman, Entrepreneur
Renowned Speaker

Lord, I pray that you take this book that you have ordained and breathe life into it. Bring it together for your glory to prove that even in our pain and darkest hours, you can still be glorified.

That I may publish with the voice of thanksgiving, and tell of all thy wondrous works.
—Ps. 26:7

Yea, though I walk through the valley of the shadow of death,
I will fear no evil: for thou art with me;
thy rod and thy staff they comfort me.
—Ps. 23:4

Fear not, for I am with you;
Be not dismayed, for I am your God.
I will strengthen you,
Yes, I will help you,
I will uphold you with My righteous right hand.
—Isa. 41:10 NKJV

CHAPTER 1

A Southern Gentleman

I met Bill when I was young and sowing my wild oats. I was 18 (the legal drinking age at the time), and he had just turned 23. We were at a club in Pasadena, Texas, called Gilley's Honky Tonk where mutual friends introduced us. I thought he was the most handsome man I had ever laid eyes on, and I wanted him.

He was tall, his posture was arrow-straight, and he strutted confidently into a room. Wherever he went, people said, "I don't know who he is, but he must be somebody important by the way he carries himself." And instead of saying, "Bill Adkins is *here*," people would say, "Bill Adkins has *arrived*."

He would be so embarrassed if he knew I was writing these things about him. They are all true, but he really was a very humble man—wise and always in control. Well, most of the time he was in control. Sometimes, at Little League baseball games, he would be so tense that it could keep your ice cream from melting in July.

I wanted to marry Bill and raise a family together. It took me quite a while to capture his heart, but I'm glad I never gave up. Our wedding cake topper was a groom trying to run away as the bride caught him by the coattails. He later told me that he was never a fast runner and that he let me catch him.

Bill was working in the oil industry in those days when we were planning our wedding. But when the industry plummeted in the early 1980s, he was laid off and had to cut back on all expenses.

Unfortunately, I hadn't purchased my wedding gown, and I had no idea what I was going to do. Then someone told me about a bridal shop that rented dresses. Renting was okay with me. I went to the dress shop and picked out a wedding dress. I was very excited that this issue had been resolved so easily—or so I thought.

The lady at the shop told me to come in the following week with my shoes so she could measure and alter the hem. I arrived a week later, and as I was being measured, I looked in the mirror and noticed a large, yellow stain down the front of the dress.

"What is this?" I asked, not hiding my shock.

"Someone rented it last weekend and spilled champagne on it," the lady said. She suggested I get a long bouquet to cover it up.

My heart sank. It was two weeks before the wedding. There wasn't time for this.

"You can pick out another dress," she said.

The majority of dresses had already been reserved, leaving only four options on the rack. I didn't like any of them. I was devastated and had no idea what to do.

So I drove to Bill's house, cried, and explained what happened. He put his arm around me and insisted I go purchase my own dress.

"We will figure out a way to pay for it," he said.

He spent his life striving to make me and so many others happy—and he succeeded time and again. On April 30, 1983, I proudly walked down the aisle to marry the man of my dreams. I was honored to be Mrs. Bill Adkins.

After we were married, Bill told me it didn't matter to him if I had worn blue jeans and a T-shirt down the aisle; I was still his beautiful bride. But he bought the dress because he didn't want me to be ashamed or embarrassed to walk down the aisle to meet him at the altar in a stained garment.

His sacrifices for my happiness demonstrated his pure and unconditional love for me. What a picture of Christ's sacrificial love for us on the cross, though we don't deserve it. "And to her was granted that she should be arrayed in fine linen, clean and white: for the fine linen is the righteousness of saints" (Rev. 19:8).

* * *

Bill was everything to me, the kind of husband I'd dreamed of having but didn't think existed. He was loving, patient, hard-working, and very protective. He made me laugh all the time. We had fun whether we were at home watching a movie, out on a motorcycle ride, or at one of the boys' baseball games.

One morning about five years before he died, I woke up and found him just looking at me. I often woke to the sound of his deep voice saying,

"Good morning, beautiful," but this particular morning he said nothing.

"What's wrong?" I asked.

He smiled. "Nothing. I'm just watching you sleep." Oh, the joy of being loved, even in the morning before you smell fresh and look your best.

How I miss the romance now. I miss waking on Saturday mornings to the smell of sizzling bacon and buttery pancakes cooking. I had to get downstairs before our teenage boys got up or I wouldn't stand a chance of getting food. Then with my belly filled and my heart full, I would put my arms around Bill and kiss him.

"Thank you," I'd say.

He wouldn't answer. He'd just smile and put his hand to my lower back, take my hand, and slowly dance me around the kitchen.

He always brought me flowers on my birthday, our anniversary, and Valentine's Day, but he didn't need a holiday for an excuse to bring me a romantic bouquet. It was nothing expensive—just a bouquet he would pick up at the grocery store and put in a vase. It brightened my whole world. One day I came home from a stressful day at work and found a beautiful flower arrangement, some Hershey's kisses laid out in the shape of a heart, and a sticky note that said, "I love you."

When our boys were little, they would wrestle each other for fun until it was no longer fun, until someone got angry and it turned into a real fight. One day, they were really going at each other. Jake was in his terrible twos and sick with a double ear infection. I had been up with him most of the night, and by lunchtime I was worn down.

When Bill called from work on his break just to say hi, I told him all three of the boys were driving me crazy, and then I burst into tears. When he arrived home, he had three beautiful roses for me. He said, "Just be patient with them, Mama. It will get better." As usual, he was right.

We often left little love notes around the house for each other. Sometimes I slipped one into his guitar case. When he opened the lid, he would smile and wink at me. Here's a little poem he wrote for me on Valentine's Day in 1992.

To My Baby Girl

I took a little time
On this Valentine's Day
To write in a poem
What I want to say

How lucky I am
To have you as my wife.
You created for me
Such a beautiful life.

So roses are red
And violets are blue;
I love when you sing
"You're Just Too Good to Be True."

Just remember that I love you
And that I always will.
You are my little girl,
And I am your Big Bill.

I Love You,
Big Bill

Chapter 2

A Brand-New Man

When Bill and I got married, we were not serving the Lord. I was raised in church, but he wasn't. I had given my heart to the Lord when I was eight years old and served God as a young person. At 16, I began working at a retail store alongside some girls a little older than I was. After work, they went out for drinks and often invited me to join them. For a while, I declined, but I enjoyed their company. So after a few months, I finally agreed to go out with them. In the beginning, I felt great conviction in my heart, knowing that getting drunk was wrong in God's eyes. But I kept going because I was having fun with them. I didn't realize how far I was drifting away from God.

Soon I quit going to church and began going to Gilley's Honky Tonk regularly, partying several nights a week. Many times, on my way out the door of my house, my mom would ask, "Where are you going?"

"Gilley's," I'd answer.

"I'm praying that God will burn that place to the ground," she'd say. There was a holy anger in her voice. In 1990, her prayer was answered. Although Gilley's had already closed its doors in 1989, it burned in 1990 and was never reconstructed after the fire. Never underestimate the power of a praying mother.

About a year after our second son was born, I felt the Holy Spirit tugging on my heart to come back to God and teach my children about Jesus. I come from a family of prayer warriors. I believe that's why I could feel the Spirit of God drawing me back to God. The thought of my children going to hell because I didn't teach them about Jesus gripped my heart.

I explained my feelings to Bill. We had been married for five years at that point, and he knew I was raised in church and that my family had deep roots in the church. However, he wanted nothing to do with it. He believed in God, but the negative example of many Christians turned him off. This was in the late 1980s when shady televangelists were being exposed on the front pages of newspapers almost every day. He didn't object to my going to church, but Sunday was his only day off, and he wanted it to be our family day. So I compromised and attended services every other Sunday. I did this for two years. During each service, I sat next to an empty chair and prayed that one day Bill would fill that empty seat next to me. I never felt compelled to talk to

Bill about the Lord. I just prayed for him and left the rest up to God.

My brother Mel was one of the greatest examples of being a disciple of Christ. He always seemed to be surrounded by the presence of the Lord. Bill enjoyed visiting with Mel. They talked about everything—sports, music, politics, and sometimes the Bible. One day after we left Mel's house, Bill said to me, "You know, when I'm around Mel, he makes me want to be a Christian." I agreed. He was a wonderful man.

As Mother's Day approached, I really wanted to go to church. I knew it was going to be a busy day. We had plans to visit my mother and Bill's mother, and celebrate me as a mother. At the time, we had our first two boys, Johnnie and Alan, and I was pregnant with Jake. I dared not ask Bill to go with me, but I wanted to let him know my desire to attend church that day. While he was out mowing the lawn, I made him a big glass of iced tea, as I often did, and insisted he take a break to cool off. While he was drinking his tea, I approached the topic.

"Do you mind if I go shopping this week and buy the boys and myself a new outfit to wear to church on Sunday?"

"Sure," he answered. "Which church are we going to?"

I was stunned. Did he just say *we*? For the past two years, I had been visiting churches but hadn't committed to any particular one. Bill mentioned a new church down the road from us that had just been built. I was so excited. The pastor of the church was a singer, and that morning he sang a couple of special songs. He had a country or Southern gospel kind of sound. He was also great on the piano. Bill really enjoyed it.

After the service, as we were walking to the car, Bill said, "If you will go to this church, I'll start coming with you."

I wanted to jump and shout. Since I was pregnant with Jake, jumping wasn't an option, but my spirit leaped for joy. For the first six months, we didn't attend regularly. Then, on a Sunday morning, one of the Sunday school teachers invited us to his class. This was the beginning of our regular attendance. Bill enjoyed the class and learned a lot.

In December 1990 toward the end of the Sunday morning service, Bill responded to the salvation invitation and gave his heart to the Lord. A couple of months after that, he was singing and playing guitar in the church's band, and he was leading worship by September 1991.

He had set aside his music for 15 years because his shift work didn't allow him to commit to a performance schedule. But now, he had a family. He had seen marriages fall apart and families destroyed because of the lifestyle of and demands on musicians. God had a place for him to use the gifts he'd put inside him. I'm forever grateful that the Lord answered my prayers for his salvation, and I'm comforted knowing that he's spending eternity in heaven and I'll get to see him again.

And they said, Believe on the Lord Jesus Christ, and thou shalt be saved, and thy house.

—Acts 16:31

Years later, my sister and brother-in-law, Joan and Randy Brewer, who were pastors of a church in Bakersfield, California, invited Bill to lead worship and also preach. Bill's sermon was titled "Our Testimony." He reminded us of how closely the world is watching us and why it's so important to live our lives in a way that won't cause others to stumble. It's ironic that the thing that turned him against Christianity was the theme of the last sermon he preached.

Bill had a beautiful, rich baritone voice with an incredible range. His singing always seemed effortless. I wanted to capture his talent on a CD, so I begged him to go to a studio and record an album. In 1996 he finally went to a local studio and recorded a professional album appropriately named *A Brand-New Man*. The song on his CD titled "The Old Man Is Dead," written by Del Way, was Bill's testimony. I remember only a couple of times that Bill could actually get through the song. He usually broke down in tears over the tender mercy of God that saved him.

Bill's father, George Adkins, had a band that played primarily country music in nightclubs and icehouses. Bill joined the band when he was 12 years old. George had a beautiful voice and was a great entertainer with a lot of charisma. Bill noticed that when George sang, people filled up the dance floor. After Bill became a Christian, he prayed that his music would have the same effect on people, except that they would fill up the altars. And they did.

In the early 1990s when Bill started singing gospel music, he was told that praise and worship is led from the keyboard and that it would not work to lead with a guitar. Well, they didn't know God's plan for Bill's life. Not only did he lead worship with a guitar, but he also taught Johnnie, Alan, and Jake to do the same. God used his style to create true worship.

We remained faithful in that church for 11 years. In 2001, the Lord led us to Crosby Church as worship leaders. I had the privilege of playing the keyboard by Bill's side. Our sons Alan and Jake were very involved in the youth band and on our team as well. As the boys grew older, they were led by the Lord to minister in other churches. Alan led worship at a church in Baytown, and Jake led worship at a church in Pasadena. At 10:30 on Sunday mornings, all three guys would simultaneously begin leading people into the presence of God—with guitars. Praise him on the stringed instruments!

CHAPTER 3

Forever Changed

The years went by so fast. The boys finished college. Johnnie and Jake were married. Alan was engaged. Bill and I began planning our retirement. Then the unthinkable happened.

September 27, 2015, was like any other Sunday, or so it seemed. We went to church. Bill led praise and worship. Then we came home and ate a light lunch. We had plans to meet our kids and grandchildren to celebrate my birthday later that evening. As we were watching a football game, Bill asked, "What's wrong with the TV?"

"What do you mean?" I asked.

"You don't see all those different screens on there?" He described it as a picture within a picture, one behind another. I told him there was nothing wrong with the TV. About 30 minutes later, he said, "I don't feel right." I jumped out of the chair and said, "Let's go. I'm taking you to the emergency room."

Bill was a big, strong, healthy man. Until now, he had no symptoms indicating that anything was wrong, no headaches, no blurred vision, no instability. We thought it would be something minor such as a pinched nerve in his neck or elevated blood pressure. Maybe his sugar level had dropped. We were not ready for the bomb that was about to fall on us.

When we arrived at the ER, I was trembling and choking back tears trying to explain his symptoms. They immediately took him for a CT scan. They saw a blockage in his brain and suspected a stroke. But he had no paralysis, numbness, or difficulty speaking. The doctor admitted him to the hospital and ordered further testing. Because there were no private rooms available, I couldn't stay with him. But I sat by his side as late as I could, went home for a few hours, and came back to the hospital around 6:00 a.m. Sometime during the night, he was taken to have an MRI. We waited and waited for the doctor to come in and give us the results. Finally, around noon the doctor came in. She showed us the picture of the MRI and said that Bill did not have a stroke, but there was a large mass in his brain.

We began asking questions until finally she said, "He has brain cancer."

The shock and disbelief were indescribable. Fear gripped us. We were totally devastated. I began hyperventilating, trying to reach for Bill's hand but unable to move because I couldn't breathe.

Bill said, "News of a stroke would be better than this report."

Our lives were forever changed. The doctor said that a neurologist would take over from here. While we were waiting for the neurologist to meet with us about an action plan, we held each other and wept. The neurologist didn't show up that day, so Bill had to spend another night in the hospital. The patient in the other bed had had his gallbladder removed and was released the next day, so I could stay with Bill from then on. I thought to myself several times how great it would be if all Bill had to worry about was gallbladder surgery.

Bill kept saying, "I love life. I don't want to die and leave my family."

The only thing I knew to do was lean on God's Word and pray for divine healing and freedom from the binding spirit of fear. First John 4:18 says that fear has torment, and we were tormented by thoughts of what was to come. We needed peace that God had everything under control, that surely

God would miraculously heal Bill so he could share his testimony of God's power.

I wanted to call our sons and our pastor so they could not only pray but also support us. But Bill didn't want anyone to know until he got home from the hospital. When we finally got home, we asked Johnnie, Alan, and Jake to come over so we could tell them the devastating news. After crying and hugging, we all settled down at the kitchen table (our regular meeting place) and began discussing the next step: seeing a surgeon and having the mass removed. Trying to calm our fears, I heard these words come out of my mouth: "This is not a death sentence. It's only a diagnosis. We will take this one step at a time." But in reality, it was a death sentence.

We shared the news with our church. Bill and I were strong believers in the power of prayer and laying hands on the sick according to scripture. "Is any sick among you? let him call for the elders of the church; and let them pray over him, anointing him with oil in the name of the Lord" (James 5:14). There were so many times in the past that Bill and I had stood with people and prayed for a miracle in their lives. Now we were the ones desperately needing a miracle. We felt our faith was being tried by fire more than ever before.

As we knelt at the altar, our pastor, Keenan Smith, and our church family gathered around us and prayed. Listening to the prayers, I thought, *Surely this is not us they are praying for.* We were worship leaders; it was supposed to be us on the platform singing songs about healing. But instead, our daughter-in-law Vasti was playing the keyboard and singing "Jesus, You're My Healer."

We determined to stand steadfast on God's Word and put our trust in the one we had prayed to for others and the healer we sang about. The army of believers covering us in prayer gave us encouragement and strength to face what was to come.

* * *

Our first step was to meet with the surgeon. On September 30, 2015 (my actual birthday), we met to discuss all our options. The surgeon said he saw only one mass that was about the size of a plum, and it was in a part of the brain that would be easy to get to. Great news!

Eager to get it over with, we scheduled Bill's surgery as soon as our calendar would allow. Alan was getting married on October 10, and we wanted to wait until after the wedding in case there were any complications during the surgery. Bill didn't want to miss the wedding or have a head bandage on in the wedding pictures. So we scheduled the surgery for October 12, 2015. The wedding was beautiful. We were so grateful to be able to celebrate with Alan and Jennifer as they began their new life together.

Monday came, and we went to the hospital so Bill could be prepared for surgery. The doctor told us the surgery would take around three-and-a-half hours. It seemed more like three-and-a-half days to me. Bill did well during the surgery. When the doctor came down the hall, I hoped to hear that the tumor was benign and gone. Our family and friends gathered around to get the report. The doctor told us that he had removed the tumor. However, lab results confirmed it was glioblastoma multiforme. I knew exactly what that was because my sweet brother, Mel Welch, had passed away on November 14, 2001, from glioblastoma astrocytoma.

There is no known cure for this type of cancer. It's very aggressive. I knew that if God didn't intervene, Bill would have only 12 to 15 months to live. This was the beginning of a very difficult, 14-month journey.

CHAPTER 4

The Beginning of the End

Bill and I began each day with prayer, anointing him with oil (sometimes, he anointed himself), declaring the Word of God, and asking for God's wisdom, direction, and healing.

> *If any of you lack wisdom, let him ask of God, that giveth to all men liberally, and upbraideth not; and it shall be given him.*
> *—James 1:5*

When Bill began radiation treatments, I was still working a full-time job. I had a very kind and understanding boss who allowed me to work from home so I could drive Bill to treatments and doctors' appointments. I'm forever grateful for the liberty he afforded me. I went into the office once a week but continued working from home until it became necessary to resign the following August. I needed all my focus on Bill.

The enormous weight of the devastating prognosis was unbearable at times. I didn't realize it before, but I had become accustomed to leaning more on Bill instead of the Lord. Now I was forced to totally depend on God. But that was a good thing. I needed Abba Father who tenderly takes care of us in times of trouble. Any little thing that went wrong in everyday life seemed multiplied a thousand times, and I was crying out to God for help more than ever before.

Each day, we faced something new. It seemed that anything that could go wrong did go wrong. First, the air conditioning in my car broke. We had to have it fixed because it was difficult for Bill to get into his truck. Next, the transmission in my car went out. Then at home, an outside water pipe burst. My washing machine broke, and it was going to cost more to fix it than it was worth. A raccoon got inside our walls. Red wasps got in our house, and we couldn't figure out how.

A jack-of-all-trades, Bill had always fixed things. He could build a wooden deck, fix a car, and repair appliances. Taking care of broken things may sound insignificant, but my priority was taking care of Bill. I didn't know where to take my car to have the repairs done or what plumbing company to call to fix the busted pipe. Who should I call to get rid of the raccoon in the wall? I didn't have time for this.

Well, things got done, and I was able to breathe a brief sigh of relief. For the next six weeks, I took Bill to radiation treatments and doctors' appointments. He completed the treatments the week after

Thanksgiving and began an oral chemo called temozolmide. Fortunately, the side effects were minimal at first. He had a decrease in his appetite but could still eat without getting sick.

When Christmas season came around, we tried to maintain as much normalcy as possible even though we knew it would most likely be his last Christmas here on earth. We had a tradition that while putting up the Christmas tree, we would listen to Christmas music and drink wassail or hot chocolate. I took a deep breath and prayed, "Lord, please give me strength to get through this." It was hard to choke back the tears as we opened presents on Christmas Day and even more difficult as we sat down to eat our Christmas dinner. But we offered up thanksgiving to our King Jesus and celebrated his birthday.

When the holidays were over, Bill started showing the side effects of the treatments. He started losing his balance and fell frequently. When his legs grew weak, he said, "I feel like I'm wearing large clown shoes and trying to walk across a mattress." He also lost peripheral vision in his left eye.

Aside from receiving complete healing, Bill's greatest desire was to continue leading praise and worship. He kept saying, "The devil isn't going to steal my worship." He would boldly walk onto the platform wearing his black cowboy boots and kick down the spiritual wall that tried to hinder his praise to God. When he struck the first note on the guitar, bam! We were in the presence of the Lord.

> *But thou art holy, O thou that inhabitest the praises of Israel.*
>
> —Ps. 22:3

Bill did well leading worship for about three months. For the first two songs, he could stand. Then he would sit on a stool to finish, and eventually he sat the whole time. Gradually, he was forgetting words and missing chords on the guitar. He needed assistance getting on and off the platform.

Eddie Dyson, an amazing servant of God, was always there to help us in any way he could. We had known Eddie and his family for many years. It was rare to ever have to ask for Eddie's help. Just discussing what we needed got Eddie on top of the task before we could blink. As Bill grew weak, Eddie was there to help him balance his guitar since Bill's body tended to lean to the left, and he would lose the strength to hold his instrument. One day I asked Bill if he could tell any difference in the way he played the guitar. He said, "Yes. The notes are not as sweet as they once were."

As Bill's strength declined, the tumor grew back. We were leaving a restaurant one evening, and on the way to the car, he fell in the parking lot. Because he could no longer get back up on his own whenever he fell, I bought him a cane and insisted that he use it. He was embarrassed to walk around with it, but it was necessary. Eventually, he needed a wheelchair and assistance to get around. It challenged my strength to maneuver him. He was a big guy at six feet two inches and 240 pounds. Once when we were getting on an elevator at the medical facility, I accidently ran him into the door. A doctor on the elevator looked at Bill and said, "Sir, are you all right?"

Bill said, "Yeah, she doesn't have her license yet. She's still trying to learn how to drive this thing."

"You'd better be nice to me," I teased, "or I'll take you to the top of a ramp and release the brakes."

Bill continued his chemo treatments, frequent trips to the doctor, lab work, MRIs, and sometimes, the ER. On one occasion, he lost his balance and fell against the side of the bathtub, fracturing his ribs. He was in a lot of pain. The ER doctor prescribed pain meds and released him. I thought, *Oh great, another pill.* Any time we mentioned some-thing unusual, the doctor prescribed another pill. I had to keep a log of which pill and what time to administer it to him. Sometimes, the doctor would take him off one pill and prescribe another one or change the dosage.

Some of the medication was beginning to upset his stomach and decrease his appetite. Most medications needed to be taken with food. Have you ever tried to get a cancer patient or anyone who is sick to eat? Usually the first thing to go with your health is your appetite. Regaining your appetite is usually a sign that you're getting better. In Mark 5:43, when Jesus raised Jairus's daugh-ter from the dead, he told her family to give her something to eat. Her hunger was a sign of good health. Bill knew it was necessary to eat so he could keep his meds down and gain strength, and he did his very best. However, sometimes he could only take two or three bites. We tried the nutrition shakes, but they were even more difficult for him to keep down.

On April 7, 2016, another MRI revealed that the tumor had aggressively grown back. After praying for God's direction, we scheduled his surgery for April 13, 2016. It went well, and his recovery was remarkable. Within a few days, he was able to walk again with his cane. On April 24, just 11 days after surgery, he was back on the platform at church with staples in his head, leading worship again. What a strong and mighty warrior! All glory, honor, and praise to the Most High God!

During that 14-month journey, there were many ups and downs and critical decisions to make. It was overwhelming. But we prayed and sought the Lord's direction for each decision.

In all thy ways acknowledge him, and he shall direct thy paths.

—Prov. 3:6

CHAPTER 5

Finishing the Race

In May 2016, Bill began a stronger chemo treatment called Avastin administered through an IV. Before each treatment, I laid hands on the IV bag and prayed that it would accomplish its purpose and not harm any other part of his body. We both believed beyond a shadow of a doubt that God heard our prayers. "The LORD hears his people when they call to him for help" (Ps. 34:17 NLT). We believed God was in complete control because we had asked him to take control. We didn't understand the process, but we trusted him even though the terrible side effects were beginning to manifest.

A few weeks after Bill began the IV treatments, I noticed that his right foot was swollen. I called the doctor, who said it could be a blood clot and told us to take him to the ER. The doctor was correct. There was a large DVT (deep vein thrombosis) in his leg. He was prescribed blood thinners to be given by shots. It was so hard for me to give him the shots. He moaned every time I stuck the needle in his stomach. Never in my life did I think I could give someone a shot, but I knew I had to do it. I also had to give him an injection of Victoza because he had type 2 diabetes.

We spent our days researching clinical trials, but his radiation, chemo, and Avastin treatments disqualified him from participating in the studies because the use of those drugs would make his clinical data inaccurate. We needed a miracle.

We decided to get a second opinion, and I set up an appointment at MD Anderson Cancer

Center in Houston. It was ranked the number one hospital in the nation for cancer care and groundbreaking research. When we arrived, I felt a ray of hope and prayed that God would reveal a treatment that would change Bill's course. God knows about every cell, vessel, and organ in our bodies and how they work. He is our Maker.

> *For you formed my inward parts;*
>   *you knitted me together in my mother's womb.*
> *I praise you, for I am fearfully and*
> *wonderfully made.*
> *Wonderful are your works;*
>   *my soul knows it very well.*
>
> —Ps. 139:13–14 ESV

After the team of doctors evaluated Bill and carefully reviewed all his tests, procedures, and treatments, they concluded that they would have treated him exactly the way Memorial Hermann Hospital was doing it. In one sense, it was a relief to know that he was getting the best treatment available, but it was also a disappointment that they had nothing more to offer. We continued to stand on God's Word and refused to give up the battle.

A few days later, Bill began passing blood. Without hesitation, we went straight to the ER. After we provided his full medical history, the attending physician wanted to run his own tests to see the size of the blood clot in Bill's leg. The blood thinner he was taking had done nothing to reduce the size of the clot, and the physician immediately wanted to insert an IVC (inferior vena cava) filter to prevent the clot from breaking loose and going straight to his lungs. He contacted Bill's oncologist to discuss the situation, but the two doctors could not come to an agreement. The oncologist felt that increasing the blood thinner would resolve the issue, but the attending physician wanted to insert the IVC filter.

We were in Bill's hospital room when the two doctors were conversing on the phone. Since I had medical power of attorney, I had to make the decision—yea or nay. With the oncologist on the phone and the attending physician by Bill's bed, I prayed loudly, "Oh, dear Lord in heaven, if I could just get two doctors to agree. Not three or four. Just two." No wonder Jesus said in Matthew 18:19, "I say unto you, That if two of you shall agree on earth . . . it shall be done for them." I had had it! I was at the end of my rope. My poor sweetheart had already been through two major brain surgeries, radiation, chemo treatments, and painful shots every day. I was not about to take a chance on having a preventable blood clot take his life. More than being concerned, I was growing angry. I felt little horns poking out of my skull.

The attending physician said to Bill, "With a blood clot that size, you're a ticking time bomb.

I'm not releasing you from the hospital until we take care of this." I agreed with him. They prepped Bill for the minor surgery, and Johnnie, Alan, Jake, and I followed him to the operating room. The surgeon was so kind. He showed us the equipment and explained how it would be done.

I was giving him my undivided attention as he explained the procedure. I glanced over at my boys—grown men by then—hoping they were catching some of the information, too. But no. What were they doing? They thought the surgeon looked like the comedian Leo Anthony Gallagher and were drawing pictures on their phone and laughing. They showed Bill, and he started laughing. If I'd had my paddle with me, I'd have popped all three of them. (I think the horns on my head just grew a little more.)

The procedure was a success, and we brought Bill home with a sigh of relief. Almost as soon as we returned home, we turned on the TV and saw commercials about a class action lawsuit on defective IVC filters. Are you kidding me?

If someone had looked down through time and shown me everything I would be going through, I would have told them, "Go ahead and bury me now because I'll never be strong enough to endure all that." I survived each day only by the strength of God. Looking back now, even knowing how the story ends, I would do it all over again. The deep love and happiness Bill and I shared during our journey was worth the deep pain. God's Word remains true.

My grace is sufficient for thee: for my strength is made perfect in weakness.
                                    —2 Cor. 12:9

About six weeks after the IVC filter procedure, Bill was still experiencing negative side effects from the treatments. His potassium level dropped, his appetite was still decreasing, and he lost 50 pounds. As he continued radiation and Avastin treatments, he developed headaches. Then, on September 21, 2016, he had a major seizure. From that time on, he was incapacitated. He could still feed himself but couldn't get up or turn himself over. Still, he wanted to continue with treatments. The mighty warrior inside him was not going to give up.

Since Bill was unable to sit up, we had to hire a transport service to take him back and forth to treatments. I'd never ridden in an ambulance before. The rides were rougher than some of the roller coasters I'd been on. God have mercy on people who are in pain and have to endure that ride. It was an out-of-pocket expense of $700 per trip. At that rate, they should have been able to at least go around one or two of the potholes for a smoother ride.

Around the beginning of November, Bill became noticeably weaker. He needed assistance eating and had lost a total of 90 pounds. His voice was so weak, eventually becoming a whisper, that I struggled to understand him. Then he struggled to breathe, so off to the ER we went again. An MRI revealed another tumor had grown around his right temple. The doctor said he could perform surgery using Gamma Knife radiosurgery. We thought it would help relieve pressure from his brain and help him regain strength as the previous surgeries had done. So we scheduled the surgery.

There was a little good news: the blood clot in his leg had dissolved. The surgery went well, but we saw no improvement as we had with the other surgeries. He could no longer swallow food or liquids. On November 17, 2016, the doctor inserted a feeding tube into Bill. He had now lost 100 pounds. After much prayer and discussion with our family and doctors, we called in hospice. What an excruciating decision!

Hospice first visited our home on Saturday November 19, 2016. Then they came to our house to evaluate him every day. Three days in, they told us to stop feeding him because his body was shutting down and rejecting it. Another heart-wrenching decision! Food restores health, and now I couldn't feed him? It was an unbearable sign of the end.

Jake and Vasti helped me as much as their schedules would allow. They had been married only three months when Bill was diagnosed. Without hesitation, Vasti was beside Jake and our family doing whatever needed to be done. They filled in as worship leaders when Bill could no longer do it. Vasti sat next to Bill's bed and sang. It was amazing how this newlywed couple spent their first year of marriage. They never complained about sacrificing their time. Vasti had one thing to focus on: standing beside her new husband to support him. She is such an amazing woman of God.

On Tuesday November 22, 2016, hospice informed us that Bill had approximately 24 to 48 hours to live. We called family and our pastor and his wife. We thought we would do what Bill loved most—praise and worship. Alan brought out the guitar and Bill's songbook. We surrounded his bed and began worshiping. I think we sang every song in the book, old and new songs, nonstop for about four hours. The presence of the Lord and his peace filled the room. Bill's eyes were closed, but I could see a lot of movement in them. I know he was worshiping with us.

The next day, Bill had rapid, labored breathing. I called a nurse from hospice and asked her to come. She tried to check his blood pressure, but it was so low that she couldn't get a reading. She told us it would be just a few more hours.

I rebuked her words. As long as he had breath, there was life and hope. We gathered around his bed, and for the next six hours, I held his hand, caressing his arm, and kissing his face. As time went on, his breathing began to gradually slow down. His body was getting cold. At 2:30 a.m. on Thanksgiving Day, Bill took his last breath here on earth. He finished the race.

Thanksgiving Day would never be the same. I looked up toward heaven and said, "Lord, couldn't you have waited one more day?" But I figured that since Bill was a praise and worship leader for 26 years, what more appropriate day for him to enter the gates of heaven with thanksgiving in his heart and into his courts with praise. He was so in love with Jesus, and he longed to see him face-to-face. I believe when he was greeted in heaven, he heard the words, "Well done, my son, welcome home."

CHAPTER 6

The Pains of Death Surround Me

We notified family and friends that Bill had passed. My heart was shattered beyond measure. I still couldn't believe it had happened. Why would God give me the world and then take it all away? I'd had it all. After a beautiful life with Bill for 36 years, I now had to find a way to go on without him. Yes, there had been obstacles and challenges in our marriage. We had disagreements and normal arguments about finances and raising children. But we were always careful with the words we used when expressing our emotions. Words are powerful, and once they've been spoken, no matter how many times you say you're sorry or didn't mean it, you can't take them back.

> *Tears blur my eyes.*
> *My body and soul are withering away.*
> *I am dying from grief;*
> *my years are shortened by sadness.*
> —Ps. 31:9b–10 NLT

I felt like someone was pounding me in the belly with a sledgehammer. It took every bit of strength just to walk across the room. Maybe it was from the physical exhaustion taking hold of my body, the sleepless nights of constantly checking on Bill, bathing and caring for his hygiene—difficult tasks because he was such a big man. It had been important to me to give him the best and most tender loving care. I don't think there are words in the English language, or any language, that can describe the excruciating pain I felt. Death on this earth makes everything seem so final, but I knew from scripture that it's not final. "Yes, we are fully confident, and we would rather be away from these earthly bodies, for then we will be at home with the Lord" (2 Cor. 5:8 NLT).

Planning Bill's memorial service felt unreal. Bill was only 59 years old. In addition to being a part-time praise and worship leader, he had worked a full-time job at Anheuser-Busch for 30 years. December 31, 2016, was the date we had set for our retirement. We had plotted so many plans over the years. His death was just five weeks before that date.

The arrangements were difficult. It was Thanksgiving weekend, and many friends and family were out of town. How do you honor such a remarkable man? He was a loving and faithful husband, an amazing father, a dynamic worship leader, and a loyal friend. He left golden footprints everywhere he went. I wanted everyone to know how wonderful he was. But in the end, the thousand people in attendance already knew how wonderful he was. That's why they were there.

Bill would have been proud to hear his sons singing and all the wonderful things people said about him as we celebrated his life. At the end of each church service, Pastor Keenan would always ask Bill to take us out with a song. At the end of the memorial service, Pastor Keenan said, "We will follow tradition and have Bill take us out with a song." The church shared a video of Bill singing "I See the Lord." Seeing him on those large screens made it feel as if he were there in person. The crowd exploded into worship and celebration. Our family was so grateful for the many people who showed up to honor Bill.

After the memorial service, many dear friends came to me to express their love. I was lost in a fog. In the corner of my eye, I sensed something like a 10-foot angel standing behind me. It was Eddie Dyson continually giving me tissues and helping me stand. Eddie was always there for Bill, and now he was there for me. I believe he will have great rewards in heaven for all those he has helped over the years.

As the days went on, the grief was settling in. My heart was aching. I'm no stranger to grief. My father died unexpectedly when I was 19 years old. Fifteen months later, my brother Dean was in a fatal car accident. I lost my mother to a stroke when I was 30 years old. I lost my brother Mel to cancer. My beloved brother-in-law Randy Brewer passed away just three months before Bill. I had also lost both my mother-in-law and father-in-law. After losing these loved ones, I found that crying released some of the intensity of the pain. Another comfort was knowing that all these loved ones were Christians and that I would see them again in heaven. But the grief I felt after losing Bill was so different. I knew it was going to take time to heal.

My soul refused to be comforted.

—Ps. 77:2

How do you comfort those who have lost someone they loved so much? As a grieving widow, the last thing I wanted to hear from people were those three little words that still make me cringe: *Well, at least.* "Well, at least he's in a better place." "Well, at least you're still young enough to get married again." I had just lost the man of my dreams. The last thing on my mind was finding another man to marry. I wasn't sure whether I wanted to scream at the top of my lungs or just throw up. Some of the things that well-intentioned people said made me so angry. I asked God if I could punch them in the mouth or at least cuss them out. I felt those little horns growing on my head again.

I realize people search for the right words or a Bible verse to lighten the sadness. But in my own experience, I've learned that sometimes the best thing to say is, "I'm so sorry" or to be silent. Just being there with a person speaks volumes. Everyone is different. You may have a good word to share, but timing is important. There's "a time to keep silence, and a time to speak" (Eccles. 3:7). Good Lord, even Job, who lost everything, including his 10 children, had a grace period. When his friends showed up, the Bible says, "So they sat down with him on the ground seven days and seven nights, and no one spoke a word to him, for they saw that his grief was very great" (Job 2:13 NKJV). Of course, when they did open their mouths, things went south. Words are very powerful. Be careful what you say.

CHAPTER 7

Walking through the Darkness

A year after losing Bill, my heart was still shattered. Even now, I don't know whether it will ever heal. I wish Bill could wrap his arms around me and tell me that everything is going to be okay. I always felt safe in his arms, but I can't reach those arms now. I need him more than ever. I need his advice. How do I live without the love of my life? I never imagined that someone could be in such extreme pain and still be alive to tell about it. I feel so abandoned. Grief is such a deep, dark pain.

All three boys had married and moved out, and Bill had passed on to heaven. I was left alone in a house that had always had a lot of activity, conversations, and music. I'd never lived alone. Everything was so quiet and lonely. There was no one to talk to, watch TV with, or have dinner with. I kept looking around the house and replaying all the memories we'd made there. We were a young couple when we bought this house. It was so exciting to move into a brand-new house. There was much joy and anticipation of raising our family there. After closing on the house, Bill and I came just to look around. He carried me across the threshold. It never crossed my mind that 28 years later Bill would be carried across the same threshold on a stretcher headed to a funeral home. The pain was unbearable.

I put into practice everything I had learned about trusting in God's Word and letting him do his perfect work. I quoted scripture to myself. I believed that "faith comes by hearing, and hearing by word of God" (Rom. 10:17 NKJV), but my faith was challenged. The days and weeks turned into months. Though I was praying and offering up thanksgiving for all the Lord had done for me, something was wrong. My heart was not healing. Rather, the pain was intensifying. My days were lonely, and the long walk upstairs each night to an empty king-sized bed was difficult. Grief was consuming me.

"Lord, I need direction," I prayed into the darkness. "I feel like I'm spinning around and can't find my way. I'm crying out to you, O Lord, for I know you will lead me out."

The valley of the shadow of death can be a very fearful place, especially when you've never been there before and you're not familiar with your surroundings. You may hear unfamiliar sounds from animals that frighten you. It may be cold and leave you feeling exposed to the elements. You don't know which direction leads out. But when you make Christ the center of your life, he will make a path in the valley and lead you in the ways of righteousness for his name's sake. He will shine a light in the darkness that gives you hope. "By his light I walked through darkness" (Job 29:3).

Where there is a shadow, there must be a light somewhere. I saw the shadow of death. Death wanted me. Thoughts of suicide flooded my mind, and the enemy tried to convince me that it was the only way to end the pain. I really didn't want to die; I just wanted the pain to die. I don't care how strong of a Christian you are, the sufferings of this world can influence your thoughts. Even the Apostle Paul said, "We were under great pressure, far beyond our ability to endure, so that we despaired of life itself" (2 Cor. 1:8 NIV). I knew there was hope in God, but I still felt hopeless because the grief process was so intense. I found myself in constant combat with these thoughts: *Just go ahead and get it over with. God's not doing anything for you. He doesn't even hear your prayers.*

I confess I entertained those thoughts because the intense pain would not ease up. But I knew God's Word and believed that even though I was walking through the valley of the shadow of death, I would only see the shadow, and that death would pass over me. At that point, I knew I had to cast down those thoughts by believing that Abba Father loves me and will come through for me. I'm still learning as I keep walking and leaving the former things behind.

I believe we can talk openly to the Lord about our thoughts and feelings. He's not a statue but rather a living God who talks back to us. God knows our every thought—the good, the bad, and the ugly. He is omniscient. "You know my thoughts before I think them. . . . LORD, even before I say a word, you already know it" (Ps. 139:2, 4 NCV).

I had many conversations with the Lord on those bleak days:

Lord, your Word says that you are nigh unto those who are of a broken heart. I am daily crying out to you in extreme pain, but I'm not hearing from you. Why are you not healing my broken heart and binding up my wounds as you said in Isaiah 61:1? I believe your Word that was taught to me since I was a little girl. Lord, you know the first scripture I memorized when I was three years old: "Even the winds and the sea obey him!" (Matthew 8:27). I believed it then, and I believe it now.

I soon realized that I didn't lose Bill. When you lose something, you don't know where it is. I *know* where Bill is. He's in heaven for eternity.

If you declare with your mouth, "Jesus is Lord," and believe in your heart that God raised him from the dead, you will be saved. For it is with your heart that you believe and

are justified, and it is with your mouth that you profess your faith and are saved.
—Rom. 10:9–10 NIV

I had heard Bill pray that prayer and watched him live a life devoted to the Lord.

Many people have told me this is just another chapter in my life. How many chapters are there? I don't know. But I'm glad to be in God's story. I may not be in the Bible, but I'm still in God's story. God knows the end from the beginning. The chapters in my life will continue until God says, "The end."

CHAPTER 8

Independence Day

After a year of sitting in a chair and crying from morning until night, I realized I was not going to figure it all out. I spent hours replaying the events in my mind. Someone once said that there is something called "paralysis in analysis," which means you can spend so much time trying to analyze God's purpose for what happened that you become paralyzed in your thoughts. I didn't need to know *why* Bill died; I needed to know why God chose that timing.

Why hadn't God allowed us time to enjoy a few years of retirement together? Bill had wanted to buy a boat. He'd often talked about fishing with our sons and grandchildren. I'm not a big fan of fishing, but I absolutely love the water. It would have been wonderful to be out on the water with him, watching him teach our grandchildren to fish. We also had many plans to travel to places we'd never been. Bill's mother, Anna Maria, was from Pisa, Italy. She married an American soldier in World War II and moved to America. We yearned to travel to Italy to see her homeland and all the sights. We often talked about how romantic it would be.

Even if I had known God's purpose, I don't think it would have healed my pain. Jesus knew why he had to die on the cross, yet he still told God that if there was any other way, to let that cup (death) pass from him. Even knowing why didn't prevent Jesus's pain or death. But God knows the end from the beginning.

You made all the delicate, inner parts
of my body and knit me together in my
mother's womb.
   Thank you for making me so wonder-
fully complex!
   Your workmanship is marvelous—how
well I know it.
   You watched me as I was being formed
in utter seclusion, as I was woven together
in the dark of the womb.
   You saw me before I was born.
Every day of my life was recorded in your
book.
   Every moment was laid out before a
single day had passed.
                  —Ps. 139:13–16 NLT

A time to be born, and a time to die.
                   —Eccles. 3:2

I was living my life under the shadow of Bill's death. I felt like David who grieved his loss in Psalm 13:1–3. I also had sorrow in my heart daily and asked, "How much longer?" The pressure was building inside me. I needed relief from the pain it took just to get out of the bed each day. I began to force myself out of the house to go shopping and watch my grandchildren's sporting events. Getting out and having a change of scenery did seem to help.

Bill and I also had plans to do some upgrades to our home in order to sell it and downsize. We didn't want to take up our weekends or vacation days working on it, so we delayed things with the intent of doing it after we retired. Instead, we decided to take a three- or four-day cruise or spend a weekend riding our motorcycle up the Galveston coast.

I was tremendously blessed that our home was paid for, and I didn't have a mortgage to stress over.

However, it was beginning to need maintenance. Not a big deal, I thought. After all, I had three grown sons to call on when needed. But I didn't take into consideration that they were married, had full-time jobs, and spent much of their time at their children's schools and sports activities. They couldn't drop everything to run and help Mom at any given time. This was a wake-up call I wasn't expecting. I was grieving. I was not in a state of mind to take care of maintaining a house.

Well, ready or not, there I was, forced to be independent. I was used to Bill (Mr. Fix-It) taking care of issues. As a stay-at-home mom when our boys were growing up, I never realized how much work went into keeping up a house. Bill's handyman skills had saved us a lot of money. We had a washing machine that lasted 18 years. The last time it broke, Bill went to get his tools to fix it. I jumped in front of it and said, "Not this time, cowboy. I want a new one." Yes, he did buy me a new one.

But now, I had more meltdowns than I could count over things that arose. Even minor things seemed catastrophic. I turned to God and cried out for help: "Lord, I pray for the courage to face the problem, find the solution to fix it, and have the strength to get it done."

After resolving matters by myself for a little while, I developed a little confidence that I could take care of things. I gradually had my kitchen remodeled, installed new floors, and painted and redecorated a couple of bedrooms. They were baby steps, but at least I was walking. I fell down a few times, but I got right back up. Although there were days that I felt—and sometimes still feel—sorrow and loneliness, my heart was healing. When we married, we became one. When he died, I felt like half of me was gone. I wanted to be whole again.

I'm learning to lean on the Lord more than ever before in every aspect of my life. Being a widow does not define who I am. I'm beginning to see hope and know that I am complete in Christ. He has been faithful to be there for me. His promise is true. "For he hath said, I will never leave thee, nor forsake thee" (Heb. 13:5). I encourage you to begin to rely on the Lord for strength, grace, and wholeness. He longs for you to trust him. I often remind myself to say this prayer:

I thank you, Lord, that you are; I'm thankful that I know you. I'm thankful that you love me. And I'm so grateful that you have blessed me with a home even if it requires maintenance. I praise you for your goodness and your wonderful works to me and my family.

What My Kitchen Table Hears

It's only a table, but that table heard so many
family conversations.
There was so much emotion and history stored in
every splinter, nut, and bolt.

It was the family meeting place. We sat there
every evening and chatted over dinner.
It witnessed everything, from the boys'
homework to the most pivotal moments of our
lives.
It's where we celebrated every Thanksgiving,
Christmas, and birthday and planned our
family vacations.

The laughter was priceless!

We often sat there for hours, talking about school,
Little League baseball, youth camp, music,
and church.

We shared our childhood memories: Bill's five-
    mile walk to school each day (that turned out
    to be only one mile).
We recalled our love story, how Bill and I met at
    Gilley's Honky Tonk.

That table heard advice, opinions, and discussions
    about which college to attend.
Graduation invitations were prepared. Wedding
    lists were written.

It heard us tell our boys about their father's cancer.
It heard us plan the funeral, held stacks of photos
    for the slide show.

It's the table where so much laughter, sorrow,
    arguments, and love abided.

The boys have all married and moved out.
Bill is in heaven.

Now it's just me and this old table where I'm
  writing—another memory in its grains.

The Lord says he prepares a table before me
  in the presence of my enemies—Sorrow.
  Loneliness. Tears. Grief.
Yet my cup runs over, for he gives laughter, joy,
  and peace.

Thank you, Lord, for this table of beautiful
  memories ingrained with the extraordinary
  life I have lived.
Thank you for your wonderful works to my
  family and me.

CHAPTER 9

Priceless Treasures

Before Bill died, the sound man at church, Bill Roberts, recorded the praise and worship time every Sunday morning. When the service was over every Sunday, he gave the CD to his granddaughter, Emma, so she could personally deliver it to Bill. She was just a toddler, and her grandfather would carry her up to the platform. Her excitement over giving Bill the CD overwhelmed his heart with love for her. As she grew older, she would run from the back of the church to the platform by herself and patiently wait for Bill to acknowledge her. She and her grandfather had no idea how the exchange of the CDs became such a precious, treasured event. She was only 10 years old when Bill passed away. The following is a monologue Emma wrote and presented in her drama class at school. It was written three years after Bill's death.

My Bill Adkins
By Emma Buchanan

I was his Emma. The one he got the CDs from every Sunday morning at church. The one he cheered for at my softball games. The one he believed in more than I did myself. The one who loved him so dearly. The one who was weeping while writing a monologue. The one who is weeping inside while performing my memories.

He was my Bill Adkins. The one who sang every Sunday morning with his guitar, praising and worshiping the Lord. The one who would give anything to be with the

Lord. The one who actually went to be with the Lord.

I loved him more than any monologue could ever attempt to say. And, hopefully he did too. I hate cancer. It takes the good people. The worthy people. The godly people. I've been told it was a good thing he passed, for now he's in heaven and his suffering is no more. I agree, but he shouldn't have been suffering in the first place. Not at all. A man like him deserved nothing but happiness.

I loved him more than any memory could ever attempt to portray. I don't even feel like this happened to me, honestly. This tragedy in my life. This triumph of his life. This is not my story. This is an era of life that happens to lots of people: death and its repercussions. But why him? Why Bill Adkins? I will never know.

I will never know.

Bill had a lasting influence on many people through his music. He would sing at local opry shows that were primarily country music, but he was considered the resident gospel singer and was very well received. He touched lives of the young and old alike.

We accumulated quite a few worship CDs over the years. One day, I began listening to them. It was wonderful hearing Bill's voice. He sounded more alive to me than ever before. It was great therapy for me. Both the hearing of his voice and the anointing that flowed through his voice were very comforting.

Listening to those CDs was like hearing from heaven. One morning, I prayed for a glimpse of Bill however God saw fit to make that happen. I should have guessed that the Lord would answer my prayers through those old worship CDs. On the CD from Crosby Church dated June 9, 2013, Bill was ministering between songs, and here are his exact words:

Holy, Holy, Holy. Blessed be the Lord God Almighty. Who was and is and is to come. That's what they're saying right now in heaven. The choir in heaven is singing Holy, Holy, Holy. Blessed be the Lord God Almighty. Who was and is and is to come. They're worshiping God all the time in heaven. So when you join in here on earth, it makes it just that much better.

I thank the Lord for hearing and answering my prayer. I thank him that he always hears me when I pray. Listening to Bill's worship CDs, I was amazed at his revelation of the throne room of God. It was ordained years ago that God would give him a spirit of worship, a spirit so strong that when listeners closed their eyes, they were in the Holy of Holies and beholding the King. In my grief, Bill was ministering healing and comfort to me through those 10-year-old CDs. God knew back then that the person he could use to help me the most would be the love of my life.

One beautiful Saturday, I was sitting on our deck that Bill built, writing about him. I wished he were there with me and thought about how much I loved and missed him, about my loneliness without him. If he were there, he would have been praying and seeking the will of God for the next morning's worship. Usually, when he finished choosing the songs, he rehearsed them. Sometimes, I would look over at him, and his eyes would be closed as he was caught up in worship. He was a true worshiper.

I missed doing praise and worship with him. I had not been back to Crosby Church since he died. It was too difficult to look at the platform and not see Bill leading worship. We were there for 15 years, and we loved our church family and our pastors, Keenan and Lorie Smith. I needed to find a new church, but I had no idea where to go.

On occasion, I visited other churches, but many times I walked away disappointed. They were good churches, and they all had a lot to offer. But I believe that God places each member in the body as it pleases him. In my opinion, that's when you are most effective. I was not feeling peace in my heart that the churches I was visiting were where God wanted me.

I was beginning to get frustrated. Although Crosby Church was my home, it was absolutely out of the question for me to step foot on the property because it was too painful without Bill. One Sunday morning, I was visiting a good church and felt that if I would give it a chance, eventually I would get used to it. That didn't happen. On my way home, I got so angry with God that I clinched my fist, hit the steering wheel, and screamed out. "God, I'm trying to get back in church and serve you, but you won't even lead me to a church!" I repented quickly. As I turned the corner of Vista Road and Space Center Boulevard, I screamed at the top of my lungs again. "Spirit of grief and spirit of heaviness, by the power of Almighty God, I rebuke you and break your back, rendering you powerless over me. The blood of Jesus is against you. You will not destroy me through grief. In Jesus's name I declare that I am free!" In a split second, I felt free. The hopeless feeling was broken off me. I felt as if I could face things with hope.

I can't remember ever feeling the power of God as strong as I felt it that day. I've been in church most of my life, and I have felt the presence of the Holy Spirit. But I don't ever remember feeling such a lightning bolt of power as I did that day.

The fear of going back to Crosby Church also broke. Immediately I said, "I'm going back home to my church." When I walked in, I felt much peace and more at home than ever before. Even with a new praise team on the platform, I was able to enter into worship. In fact, I was so proud of the team and the way they were singing high praises to the King of kings. I love my, my church. (There is a story behind "My, My Church." Maybe I'll explain it in my next book.)

I kept thinking back on the power of God I had experienced while driving down the road that day. How was it different from other times when I'd prayed with such passion? I felt it was more than a breakthrough. It was powerful. I remember asking the Lord what it was that I had experienced. He answered, "It was a resurrection-power miracle." Immediately I knew what he meant. Seven years earlier, on March 13, 2011, one of the overseers of Crosby Church was teaching about Lazarus's resurrection. He mentioned Jesus's love for Lazarus and his sisters, Mary and Martha, and he emphasized their love for Jesus. Then he explained that we are not immune to death, and at one point, he spoke directly to me. "Karen, what you need will only come by the resurrection power." I wasn't sure why he specifically spoke that to me, but having trust in this man of God, I received it as a word from the Lord.

Three hours after that service, we received word that Bill's mother had passed away. We went to the hospital and into her room. The words he spoke to me kept going through my mind. I kept wondering, "Does this have anything to do with resurrection power?" It turns out that it didn't.

However, seven years later, I understood exactly what it meant. That's what I experienced that day in my car. Why was it spoken to me seven years ago? I don't know. But I do know that when God resurrects something, no one can get credit for it except God. I do give him all the glory, honor, and praise for his resurrection power. I believe the resurrection power miracle that released my hopelessness happened so I could go home to Crosby Church.

As I thought back even further to November 14, 2001, I remembered a guest singer in one of our Wednesday night services. I can't remember the name of the song, but it was about Jesus's raising Lazarus from the dead. People were enjoying the song so much that the singer sang it about three times. Two-and-a-half hours after that service, I received word that my sweet brother Mel went home to be with the Lord. I think the next time someone begins to preach about Lazarus, I will have to slip out of the service. Ha! Thank God for the resurrection power of Jesus. He is the resurrection and the life!

CHAPTER 10

A Seed Reserved

I believe that long before Bill died, God took a seed and set it aside for me. He reserved a seed so I could have something to start over with again. He knew I would need it to survive the next season of my life. I've taken this tiny seed and planted it in good ground. How do I know for sure that Crosby Church is the place to plant the seed? First, it is where God told me to plant it. Also, I know that it's good, rich ground. The church is alive. I've been there for years and have witnessed a lot of things behind the scenes. We have a pastor, staff, and leaders who walk in integrity. They have a passion to reach lost souls and please our most high God.

When I returned home to Crosby Church, Pastors Keenan and Lorie Smith insisted that I sit in the front with them. I was honored. (Actually, at first, I felt like I was in the principal's office). Standing on the front row worshiping the Lord was very special.

After church one day, someone told me that the way I supported the new worship leader and how gracefully I accepted him really blessed them. I wasn't trying to prove anything; I was at peace. Deuteronomy 34:5 says that when Moses died, the children of Israel wept for 30 days, and then the weeping and mourning ended. I thought, good Lord, they only got 30 days to mourn? Joshua 1:1–2 says, "The LORD spake unto Joshua the son of Nun, Moses's minister, saying, Moses my servant is dead; now therefore arise, go over this Jordan." I don't mean to sound morbid or disrespectful to

Bill, but I felt like God was telling me, "Bill my servant is dead; now, Karen, arise, go over the Jordan." Someone told me that they really missed me on the praise team. I responded, "I'm still on the praise team. I'm just not on the platform."

The Lord is my shield and the lifter of my head (Ps. 3:3), but I've learned that before he becomes the lifter of my head, I have to become the lifter of his name in praise. I feel like I've been kissed by Jehovah, my master. Jesus is the lover of my soul. I love him with all my heart, soul, mind, and strength.

My commission from the Lord is Nehemiah 2:18: "Let us rise up and build." I will rise up and rebuild my life. But I will not build it around grief and sorrow. I will build it around righteousness, peace, and joy in the Holy Ghost.

Jesus replied, "You do not realize now what I am doing, but later you will understand."
—John 13:7 NIV

It's Morning Time

Sorrow may last for the night, but joy comes in
   the morning, Psalm 30:5 says.
But how long is the painful night going to last?
Sleep won't come, so I lie in the dark, believing I'll
   never see morning again.
I cry out to God with no answer.

What about his promise to heal the
   brokenhearted and bind up their wounds?
I'm waking in mourning, with no morning in
   sight.

Then suddenly comes a touch from heaven.
The sun shines brighter than the brightest
   noonday sun.
It's morning time!
Morning time has brought me rest. Jesus has
   wiped away my tears.

Now I know that in his tender way, he led me at
   midnight,
By his beautiful moonlight 'til the morning time
   arrived.
He hid me in a holy place, protected by his
   amazing grace.
Great is his faithfulness.

He took my brokenness and pain to glorify his
   name.
Each new morning when I wake, I pray,
Lord, help me to do with you what I cannot do
   without you.